Catherine's STORY

CATHERINE RENT

authorHOUSE®

AuthorHouse™
1663 Liberty Drive
Bloomington, IN 47403
www.authorhouse.com
Phone: 1 (800) 839-8640

Published by AuthorHouse   12/09/2016

ISBN: 978-1-5246-5458-0 (sc)
ISBN: 978-1-5246-5457-3 (e)

Print information available on the last page.

Any people depicted in stock imagery provided by Thinkstock are models,
and such images are being used for illustrative purposes only.
Certain stock imagery © Thinkstock.

This book is printed on acid-free paper.

Because of the dynamic nature of the Internet, any web addresses or
links contained in this book may have changed since publication and
may no longer be valid. The views expressed in this work are solely those
of the author and do not necessarily reflect the views of the publisher,
and the publisher hereby disclaims any responsibility for them.

CONTENTS

INTRODUCTION

M y book is written with conceptual and experiential headings for the pages I write. It is about my life, who I am and what I have done. But, mostly, it is about my experiences and my insights in later life. I try to stay in the NOW so that I can capture how I think and feel at the moment in relation to those events. This is in line with psychology and my intentions to heal myself progressively as I relay my experiences and speak them (write them). It is a form of journaling. Through journaling I come to terms with myself and others, and attempt to document who I am at any given time. This gives me perspective on my influences and state of mind during certain timeframes and encounters. I am organizing it in the form of a booklet for presentation, as I wish to share my insights.

I am basically recounting my experiences as I have them. I usually end up analyzing another person as I go into relationship rather easily, or at least I used to. I am more on guard at my age, realizing a greater purpose exists, so my choice to focus on writing and introspection makes sense. I can speak directly to my audience without knowing them personally or getting involved. I can then focus on my work until it is outlined and defined clearly. I am including my relationship with myself and my past. Information in this booklet will cover my influences primarily in the current year as I look back on relevant factors related to the experience I am currently having.

My relatedness with my family is a key to my life. So, they will be an integral part of my observations, in terms of how I relate to them. My mother has passed on, and I will mention her only briefly. My siblings and others in my life mostly seem estranged from me, or did, until I reached out. The closeness of a relationship does not seem to exist on a regular and consistent basis, and when it does I seem to have to monitor the relatedness continually to gain the results that are desirable. I am making an effort to share some of my insights with my family as my contribution to helping the family have inclusion. Perhaps sharing who I am and how I think will bring my family closer together with me. I remember earlier days where we all shared camaraderie, and I feel it is a worthwhile experience to bring back into my life.

CHAPTER ONE

Highlights of My Life

WRITE A BOOK

This is how I started. I wanted to write a book. Then, I had the thought to write an autobiography. I can then speak from my own experience without necessarily having to be an authority on a subject. I can tell my life story in an interesting way to make it saleable. That is the advisement I thought, and my intent here: to write my life story in booklet form so as to share the insights and understandings that are developing on a day to day basis given my introspection of my past and present, and of my own self. I received my Bachelor of Arts degree in Psychology in 1997. This is the psychology I practice, on myself, informally.

In 2001 my thoughts were on how institutions in the social hierarchy are organized to help us. What then is missing, I thought? How we need to reconnect after our children are grown, and rearrange our roles and usefulness so that our lives are more fulfilled in later years. Mostly, I focused on who to communicate with to work through this and where to go to establish new roles and friendships that might reflect who I am grown to be. Unfortunately, I found homelessness, and then fortunately, housing. I am regrouping.

I understand now that I was trying to grow up and be successful at something. That did not happen, and I did not have the supportive ground to coach or assist me, knowing what I was going through. We have to raise ourselves, is my thought now. We are on our own, and our best resources are the communication efforts with all the people we befriend and share our story with. Our families and friends are not necessarily equipped to deal with our professional lives as adults, unless it is specifically their vocation as well. So, it is not that unusual to gain an education and thereby create a communication gap with others as a result. This is an ongoing part of learning what to do, by knowing what we can't do, or what not to do.

I am still working on who to talk to in depth, so I type and write this journal. I want other people to know that they are not alone, and that it does matter who you talk to and what you talk about. This is part of our learning to shape our individuality and yet learning to stay within the group so as to maintain the acceptance we so need. I find in relationship that remembering the words I speak is helpful to my integration of self. Yet, also, I know that awareness that the person I am with is present and hearing and what they say is important as well. Reflection and focus on what I say and what others say helps me know what I am actually working on, beyond what my thinking mind thinks. So, I spend time in quite solitude and contemplation for parts of my day to be sure I am focused on what is important.

It is also important to develop an awareness of what projections are being put on other persons in our lives. Projections occur due to unfinished business with an earlier person, or due to fear, or need to use another to hide ourselves. Projections also can be family of origin in nature, in that our parents, and siblings, and friends are relationships that are meaningful to us. What we are projecting onto others will give us an indication of the emotional work we are dealing with that needs to be resolved. We invest emotional energy into those relationships that are the most meaningful to our survival, on physical, emotional, and mental levels. If it is with our parents, then our friends and others will reflect that. We are more than likely trying to reduce conflict with those we love.

Now, in 2016 it dawns on me, that I am re-patterning myself given different parameters. My old self is no longer needed, so I find a new self emerging with attributes that I never thought would develop in me. The miracle of it is that I have gained the ability to communicate with others in a better way. This is something I have struggled with my entire life. Then, recently, I changed. I know it must be a culmination of things that happened to develop the new quality in me, however, I cannot account for it. It is the closest thing to a miracle that I have ever experienced, and it is so simple. Give to others, and they return by giving. I am giving in my communication by listening and hearing and acknowledging that another person is present. My words and attitude reflect that I am aware and interested in their presence. The additional ingredient, perhaps, is a quality of love that is transmitted by the spirit. I am enjoying the new experience of it, like a child delighted in a new venture.

I am working on my energy level, and finally remember the adrenal glands and how tired I become if they get overstressed. So, I am taking pills to help remedy that with the hopes that my energy level will be helped by it. The B vitamins weren't enough, because fatigue still set in. This is what I am working on given my physical age of 61 years.

My apartment is reorganized in a depth-perception way, and I love it. I love living here because of it. Different patterns, textures, and colors, and shades of colors, and bright colors, and posters and pictures on the wall, framed and beautiful, with nice furniture that is attractive. Finally, my apartment feels like I am special. That is important. I never felt so special as I do now, and my apartment reflects that.

CHAPTER TWO

My Life

MY LIFE

My parents are Baptists from the South. My family and I, however, were raised in New Jersey, on the east coast of the United States, and we moved to Texas as teenagers. Being frustrated with Texas, I visited New Jersey off and on for years, and finally, (since my parents were divorced), at age 23, I visited my father who was living in Cambridge, MA with an adopted daughter. He hired me to work with him in a family business, so I lived in the Boston, MA area for a year or so.

I eventually found my way back to Texas, where my mother and siblings were. I married, had a child, and attended a community college with the lofty idea of getting my PhD in Psychology. After two years of school, working fulltime and part-time, living as a family, and as a single parent, I traveled to California where my son's dad went to live. Boys need their fathers, and my son was eight at the time. I rationalized the idea, and later, as a mother parent, fully and completely regretted it. I attended college, though, and found great work as a bookkeeper. I did, however, lose the closeness with my son. I found new friendships, and church social events that intrigued me. I stopped smoking cigarettes and started exercising: bicycling to clear my lungs and hiking for the cardiovascular workout. I then moved to northern California to finish my degree.

Because of the expense involved, and the student status I now had, I rented a room for my living arrangement wherever I went, and worked temporary jobs. My credibility waned as I had withdrawn my commitment from fulltime work to the necessary focus school requires. At the end of school, I had what is referred to as a nervous breakdown, and I ended up on medications and in a halfway house for med stabilization. I returned home to Texas for this and my family helped support me for a while. I returned to work in the temporary job market, thinking I would go to graduate school. My student loans were now due, however, and I had to earn enough to pay them. I couldn't. So, I headed to other cities with a better pay scale to attempt to pay my loans. I was unsuccessful, yet now knowledgeable and realizing my interests in leaving Texas to find a compatible living environment.

New Jersey was just a memory now, and California was beyond my cost range. I ended up in Houston, Texas, and then California, again. I knew no one so I headed home again after nine months, and eventually to California, where my son and his dad lived. I stayed there for a while, and filed for disability and public welfare. I eventually relocated to Colorado Springs, CO, and then to Memphis, TN as I headed toward Florida. From there, I decided that I needed to go back home. I was traveling too much and not accomplishing enough. I moved into an apartment complex that was affordable and laid in bed for months at a time. I was depressed; my situation got the best of me. I didn't know where to turn.

I ended up in a relationship where acceptance was the issue. It was surprising to me, but the lesson seemed to be me accepting who I am. Now, I thought, I did accept myself just as I am, so what was I fighting, and why? That is how it is in the inside of our thinking. When we view the full picture, we realize that others see us differently than we see ourselves. Also, if we can objectively notice our own failings, we can learn about ourselves. Somehow, though, it takes a relationship to bring all this about, so we can hear it from another, perhaps.

My mother died a few years earlier, and I began talking with my sister to help me work through an understanding of it. That was helpful, and I gained insight on my sister as well. We met on similar ground, analytically and otherwise to have our conversations. She, however, stays on that analytical ground, whereas I tend to shift into a spiritual, or emotional social space. That is one basic difference between us. I guess the acceptance issue I grappled with was my mother's death. Then, my sister's personality was the focus for some time while I learned about her. Sometimes acceptance is about moving forward, and in doing so, we learn about ourselves. I learned about life, and had to share it and discuss it until it was fully integrated into the person that I am, and accepted. That is the acceptance that I experienced, and my sister helped me through it. I am thankful to her for it. I now accept my mother's death, and as a result, I view my father's old age differently. I view my siblings and their importance in my life differently, and I am proceeding forth differently.

Now that I have said all this, and acceptance and differently are in my vocabulary, I realize that an explanation of the symbolic aspects of my parents needs to be said. My mother represented to me a home to go to. I could visit home by visiting her and know that all was right with the world. She wasn't the best mother, but she offered that environment for me. I think I underestimated her contribution in my life by knowing and dwelling on her shortcomings. Don't we do that even when we love another person? When she died I had to come to terms with not only her value in my life, but the fact that she was no longer available to go to. My mother was my security blanket, and I found that even as I rejected her, I was always drawn to return to see her. This is the nature of motherhood.

Now, my father is a different story. My parents were divorced when I was seven years old. I was raised by my mother, however, my father represents the development of intellect and industry in my life. I go to him when I feel that my needs in society aren't met, and I need advice. I also find that since I am or was insecure growing up, that my father acted as a surrogate mother as well. So, I would come to him with all my troubles and cry because he was willing to hear me out, and then he would proceed with his advice. In those exchanges, I learned who he was, and learned how I wanted to emulate him. I didn't want to be like my mother necessarily; I wanted to be like my father. He was intelligent and verbal and I knew I needed to learn how to verbalize my thoughts and feelings if I were going to be satisfied with my own communication attempts, and with my relationships in life.

Now, that my mother has died, by establishing a relationship with my sister, I feel I have replaced my mother with my sister. Their styles and personalities are entirely different from each other, so I still had to get over my mother and the security she offered. Just the same, I am thankful for my sister and the emotional security she offers. The main learning here, though, is that of the mortality of our parents. It is because of my mother that I don't want to take my father for granted. Now, this is precarious ground, if I am to also negotiate growing into an adult without the comfort and security of deferring to my parents. However, my father is 82 years old, and I am wanting to prepare myself mentally for his old age and passing. These are things society does not talk about that often. And, granted, my father wasn't too keen on the conversation either. But, it has to be said, and my mindset about this subject is important to me.

So, perhaps what I did was accept my mother's passing, and then prepare mentally for my father's passing, to then pave the way metaphysically for my own growing up, in the present moment, rather than in some delayed future day.

The goal is now to understand my father from his perspective. When approached regarding his age and passing, he was in denial as if we children weren't affected at all by his existence, or passing.

It is as if all should happen the way it does, and don't worry about things like that. Let us pacify Catherine from worrying about such a thing, yet I know the basis of it is more of a control issue. Just the same, how can I come to terms with something I can't even address, or confront? And, how can I then grow into the adult person who is capable of handling such things?

I feel invisible, with vague thoughts and feelings until I assert myself to communicate each and every precise thought and feeling. Even then, I have to work at the thoughts and feelings continuously until I feel certain that I am addressing the issue at hand. My family is like this as well, and for that reason, I am fortunate to be able to come to them in conversation and say some of what I think. I don't want a power struggle, or a parent-child confrontation; I want a conversation with thinking adults discussing important family issues. My family has started to meet me there so I can work at trying to maintain this level of communication with them.

I have spent years as a bookkeeper, manually and on various computer systems, so I tend to focus and then reflect and meditate. That, in itself, changes the quality of person that I am. I used to love to write poetry as I daydreamed during the lunch hour. I observed those around me, yet withheld judgment and description even to the extent that I did not have a sense of who they were. I focused primarily on details, and then concepts. I am only now really beginning to learn to understand the nature of the other person's motives, purpose and intent, and then, their choice of interrelationship. Many times I go through the relatedness with an individual, and then phase them out to reflect on what the learning was. My latest understanding is that others are drawn to reflect ourselves in some way. If perturbed with them, then we are perturbed with ourselves, or that experience would not be drawn to us. It must already exist in our psyche.

These are truisms that do not sound true or even seem true sometimes on the mental level. In fact, there is much denial about this sort of thing. When I find myself in denial, I try to approach it to work through it. I ultimately recognize the denial as an indication that the phenomenon mentioned is true and I must be at odds with it. Perhaps I don't wish to reveal myself so denial serves as a defense, or my parent's teachings are in my thinking saying other than what my inner voice says. Whatever the reason, it can be cleared out of the way for our truth to be present. We can be free of denial. This is important in that we gain an opportunity to know ourselves better, thus enabling us to help ourselves better. This makes us more capable of understanding and helping others, instead of causing the crazy-making that we typically do when we don't understand properly. Like society says, be part of the solution, not the problem. Society needs our help, too.

CHAPTER THREE

Psychological Insights

SOCIALIZING

I wanted to socialize by communicating with my family and others on Facebook. My personal page wasn't enough. I wanted to write from my higher self, not from what I call my personality self. So, I started a new page, and I opened it to the public. Here are some of my writings on my Facebook page,

What's mine? What's yours? How do we create our reality? Or, are you dissing me? This basically is my attempt at trying to understand the nature of reality, more specifically, my reality. I know that I feel one way one time and another way another time, and used to be influenced easily when growing up. Now, my question is, am I giving into the idea of others or am I working through a new way of dealing with my environment? I guess I have to know my own mind to continue.

These are the concerns women deal with that relate to boundary issues. Mostly women, I think, because women stereotypically have a lesser role than men, in that they tend to serve given the childbearing and child-raising parenting role. This isn't a lesser role overall, yet in the workplace, or other places where men thrive, it is. Men have their agendas, their arenas, and women serve a domestic purpose in most cases. Women also tend to merge with men, and lose their personal identity more easily than men. This is the boundary issue I speak of.

For boundary issues, my advice to myself and others is to acknowledge the people in your life, one by one, noticing the influencing factors of their unique being and their unique environment. Then, remind yourself of who you are and the core being that exists independently from them. Influences may be present, certainly similar DNA exists; however, be sure to know that in the core of your being is an expression that is fully you. That is ideal for you to express, for the autonomy and full power of the being that you are. Expressing another person's stuff will not necessarily empower you, and eventually you will have to come to terms with low self-esteem and manipulation in order to find your way out and back to your real self. More than likely, you were in relatedness with another for the purpose of understanding them. Let others go periodically to review where you are if you must.

Lean into it if there is a nagging issue so that you can work through it to resolve it in your life. Those attachments of need are false, and should be attended to, so they can heal and be released from you. The need attachments are our human bonds with others, and they should be nurtured and understood, but they shouldn't work against us. Know this and know the source of any attachments so you can understand yourself and your agreements with others. Don't ignore or minimize it. Try to stay out of denial as well, and keep a sense of integrity about yourself. Don't feel sorry for another, for that does not help anyone, and know you may be feeling sorry for yourself. Acknowledge that and know that is what the other chooses to do and be at this time. Your responsibility is to yourself, and the life that you create for yourself. Do not base it on pity or sorrow. Lean into that by focusing and understanding, to heal its effect on you so you can move forward to emerge with a healthy outlook.

Others are a choice. Make sure that choice is one that serves you and the other, for the best good of all. And know that if these circumstance come your way, others may be reflecting your weaknesses, or strengths. Weakness are almost as valuable as strengths in that they point the direction for your work, or at least for your understanding of what they represent in your psyche. Reflect and pay attention to what messages you consider relevant to your own psyche work, for that is the path hopefully you are choosing. Others are there for a reason, but you are in charge of you. We are not alone existentially, however, we do go it alone at times to come to an understanding of ourselves, amidst the craziness of the outer world, and its diversions and distractions. Just know you are not alone in going alone, and be thankful to work through your stuff and any craziness you encounter.

On a personal level, I have internalized the communications of a relationship from my past, and I just woke up from it by reviewing and rereading passages of my writings until I attained an understanding of essentially what I was trying to say. Then, I realized that I was reviewing my friend's experiences in his state of mind, and having shifted out of his space, I could more clearly see it. I apparently internalized some of his stuff in the course of my relationship with him, and in later years, our friendship. This is hypothetical, since I am not really sure. It is my interpretation of how, in a spiritual mindset, to advise others. Perhaps I had him in mind due to his spiritual nature.

BOUNDARIES

Here is another approach to the issues of boundaries and what's yours and what's mine? Look at the content, and recognize the significance of others and their influences on you. I was in denial about that which tells me I must have needed that connection with my friend for some reason, and/or his ego for my own personal ego needs. This I must consider. Reacting and responding from our own being is what it always seems like. We are in reaction to and response to the stimuli of the environment and others all of the time. With all the myriad of factors involved in our day to day reality we seldom question our existence, and its nature. We assume and presume and continue on our way.

Yet, these issues exist. I think especially so when our needs are unmet and our esteem is low. We then find others we can attach to, to fulfill our needs. That then causes us to further not like ourselves, and to further desire to be another. It may play out as a desire to have another in terms of a relationship, but essentially it is a desire to be another. This is especially so if messages cued to us indicate that our behavior is undesirable or our traits are disliked, or if we are struggling with self-acceptance issues. Others seems so animated, and that gives us hope that we, too, can be animated and liked.

ADVICE TO OTHERS

Counseling others can be helpful. Counseling is prevalent, in terms of advisement of what to do and how to, or where to, in a general, sociable kind of way. It is a way of having continual communication so that we stay in the loop of society. We all advise each other every day. It is part of our cultural human contact, and it is how we learn from each other. It is also vital to learn to recognize what others want from us since we are vulnerable to naivete. Our understanding of our roles and norms in society help guide our choices. People generally are not explicit about the purpose of their interactions, and much guesswork exists. Our own motives should be questioned as well for a more thorough understanding of our choice of interactions. Society is explicit and warnings abound, however, we must still go out there and negotiate the reality at hand, given all this.

Others provide feedback to our reality. They show us what we need to know and do. Recognize the reflections that they are, and understand that there is something to understand. Listen to hear, and do not underestimate yourself or others. They are present moreso than it appears at times. Their spirits exist and they are perceptive on that level, not just the mental level that they communicate from. Tune into what others are experiencing once in a while to truly understand the relationships that you are encountering and the nature of same. Don't lose yourself there. Learn to distance yourself enough to maintain objectivity should higher level learning be necessary. This will only strengthen your relationship in time, due to the needs that we have for an overview of our behaviors and choices.

If you listen and truly hear, then tuning in won't be so necessary. This is what women do, and perhaps why boundaries are our issue. Men typically protect themselves and focus on goals and self-serving interests to move forward more quickly, whereas women tend to spend time socializing to gain an understanding of what the other person is about. Realistically, though, I think both male and female tend to integrate these aspects into the personalities that we are.

Be sure and pay attention to the other person, if they are present with you. Withdraw your attention if it is uncomfortable or not aligned with your purpose as you perceive it. That will clue you as to what is you, and what is the other person's. Two people are present, but only you are responsible for you. The other person has their own agenda and set of parameters and guidelines; you have yours. If you forget yours, due to low self-esteem or other reasons, learn to remind yourself daily in your own environment and space, then vocalize same in another person's space and environment until it is who you are, and you know that you know yourself. Then you can trust yourself and others because you are fully in charge of your choices. This is maturity. Techniques such as repetition of goals, and ideals help us remember our way. All this is about parenting ourselves as adults. All this is important behavior to understand in the defining of our lives for the happiness we expect.

INCLUSION

Today was a beautiful day. It rained and cleared the air. I cried after reading an article on hub.com where a counselor in San Francisco talked about her efforts at maintaining a counseling office, showing she was good enough to earn money for her work. She used the word inclusion. My tears were of relief due to the comfort of knowing that another shares my feelings of the value of inclusion and the struggle for the worth of earning money for our knowledge.

Inclusion was what I talked about the night before in a conversation with my father. Our family lacked inclusion, not on my father's side necessarily because he included the church in his repertoire, but on my mother's side where the goal was to find a husband and make a home. My parents were divorced, separated by the time I was seven years old. I never really understood until later, while grieving my mother's death, what inclusion was. Now I understand that the element of inclusion was what I was missing all along. I think my mother made up for it on a personal level or it wouldn't have been revealed to me at that time.

Inclusion is the action of including or being included within a group or structure. Inclusion with the female, or mother parent, might mean belongingness in the family structure, at home and in social events. Inclusion with the male, or father parent, might mean inclusion at the workplace in a position of competence and worth, as well as other places where men compete. I feel I should have been included in the activities of others in my life. For instance, my relatives, my friends, and social networks at school. The inclusion I did experience was purely on a superficial level so that true belongingness didn't really develop with friends or relatives. I did establish that bond with my mother, though, and I felt that I truly belonged there when I visited her. That feeling transferred to my marriages, yet I needed more. I guess I missed my father, and his influence on my upbringing. I needed to move out of the home on my own to experience the challenges life offers. So, I did move on, and invariably, that leads me to my father.

I am jealous of my father in some ways. He reflects some of the values I have been frustrated with in my life. He is surrounded by books in his personal space, and I feel that I should have more books in my life. At the same time, I am aware of the unrealistic idea that this is. I am not interested in competing with him. He is already better than I am, academically and it is evidenced in his surroundings. I know this, and yet I also feel like I like myself better than I like him. So, I feel my ego is intact with this. I may, however, be trying to measure up in order to enter his sphere of influence, and ultimately, gain his approval. I am sure this is from my childhood, growing up without him. My parents were divorced, so I don't have a lot of ingrained manipulative personality aspects that reflect his environment. I am, however, his child, and I do have intuitive aspects of how to proceed. I guess I am saying I require his attention and approval, and my efforts demonstrate that. I am, however, also aware that I am not willing to lose myself to gain that approval, and that as an adult, the approval I require moves into the public ground, on professional and societal levels.

BACK TO WHAT'S MINE?
WHAT'S YOURS?

The boundary issues have surfaced again. In analyzing and reflecting on my reality, it seems clear to me that I have taken on some of my father's stuff. I say stuff because it is a combination of thoughts, words, and feeling that seem to belong to him. This I base on my hearing him say the words that reflect those thoughts and feelings, assuming that they are actually feelings and not defenses. Then, I have an awakening, and think that he is like the wizard in the Wizard of Oz, and he is saying words that are not indicative of the true feelings behind the mask.

I take things personally and think others think I am not interesting enough to get involved. Then, I don't think the family is interested enough in me to get involved in my work. My spiritual thinking tells me to look at my thoughts so that I do not judge without looking at myself first. If I think about the words that my family isn't interested in me, I find I am wrong. My family does show some interest in my work. Why am I deluded? My sister read my 100 page journal with its wanderings and yet I act as if she wasn't interested. She was, and we talked about the journal, and my wanderings. So, for me to think otherwise, is some kind of misunderstanding. I can't take that stance; it doesn't serve me. It also doesn't reflect my reality, in truthfulness.

My father does, however, seem to be reflective of me. I never thought of the parallels until now. I read in a social psychology text where it is common for us to view others as a mirror in order to understand ourselves better. This is what I seem to be doing, although, admittedly, my interest is elsewhere now that I have decoded his emotional importance to me. Perhaps much of it was curiosity.

Thinking of my self in this way took some reflection, for my mind initially viewed reality through defenses and expectations. I understood others in a direct way through their spoken words. However, I wasn't seeing the actual reality that was presented before me. I was caught up in my own needs as well. Now, as I view the defenses projected with words, the wizard in the Wizard of Oz comes to mind again. I am learning to understand reality in this way. This is important because I am a reflection of my parents regardless of what defense or image is put up. I am a part of the human family, and this is our nature so it must be understood. (Am I the last one to know, or is my vulnerability because I am a woman in society? I am referring to the reality behind the façade that is what I haven't been interacting with.)

WIZARD OF OZ ALLEGORICAL INTERPRETATION

As these ideas come to mind, I think of the wizard as he puts up a front to scare Dorothy and her friends away. The wizard finally shows his vulnerabilities when Dorothy dispels his mask, and he offers the few things he can, a medal for courage, a heart for love, and a diploma for attainment of thinking. All these reflect his acknowledgement of their journey and the fortitude required to meet him. He is just like a father in charge of his castle requiring worth to be proven and then rewarded, only tempered with love and humility. This is not stated, much as others don't outright state their reality. I have to hear words for a while, and guess, and introspect. Are others even in touch with their reality? I want others to say their truth so I can know. I feel that I have earned and deserve the respect for being a human being in the world. That is not too much to ask, for certainly I love and respect others. I lifted the screen and saw behind the mask, and now I understand vulnerability. I also understand Dorothy and the Wizard of Oz better.

The witch in the castle represents the mother, after the seasonal harvest. The leaves are falling from the trees, and the gremlins of winter are surrounding the castle. The witch is exiled to the far reaches of the kingdom where she will not interfere with the ruler-ship of the kingdom probably after the harvest, when she bore a son for the king. It is all a symbolic representation. Mother is no longer needed in a man's world. She has met her requirements and since her day is over, it is now about Dorothy's journey.

Dorothy visits her and is brought into her plight. Dorothy soon thereafter flees with her life to venture to the castle of the king, the father, to regain some authority, strength and power. His servant answers and eventually sheepishly offers the medal, heart symbol and diploma. These symbols could be medals of war, heart symbols of fencing, and a deed of land, or proclamation from France, or another country. In any case, he sends her on her way as she must return home. These affairs of state are not the affairs that should concern her.

Dorothy wakes up, as if from a dream, and is greeted by the ordinary folk in her environment to show she must be content with the life she has. Perhaps they are commoners serving the kingdom, or she is the prince destined to live among them until their needs are attended to by the king and the kingdom. That would explain why she is drawn to find her own heritage, perhaps knowing of her noble birth, or just knowing that something more must exist. Or, perhaps she is driven merely to seek a better life.

Questioning things, and venturing forth to explore new ground isn't the objective the kingdom wants from their commoners. We must accept what we have and not talk about or explore new options. It all starts because Dorothy's pet dog, Toto, goes into a neighbor's yard and disturbs the garden. The garden of Eden is disturbed if commoners venture into it. Their eyes may show desire at seeing the sparkle of another's good, such as the sparkly effect of the red shoes Dorothy gets from the Good Witch of the North. She is the good mother saying that Dorothy can have the riches of the kingdom. The Wicked Witch shows Dorothy what could happen to her, and essentially plays the dual role of the executioner during the Spanish Inquisition. The story is a parable yet it is also representative of the way of life of medieval times. There is much hope shown in Dorothy's receiving of the shoes.

Dorothy may be representative of women in puberty when they seek out new counsel for the new journey, with the blood of her puberty represented by her red shoes, and the house fallen on the witch as representative of the life she is leaving behind. She must go forth and reckon with her new reality. Earlier she is trying to balance on the fence, showing she is growing up to a taller, bigger self. She falls, and they show pigs fenced in. The garden is in the neighbor's yard, not hers. She is surrounded by three working men, hardly the choice of marital partners for a young lady growing up in their midst. She probably wishes for a prince, and ultimately becomes representative of the prince as a dual role by entering the castle. Her friends are representative of the three men working on the farm, showing their lack of brains, courage, and fortitude. This is what she must negotiate, for they are there and so is she. Aunt Emma is merely caretaker, and the witch on the bicycle that takes Toto is only there to taunt her as if to say she is not good enough. The men workers lack manners, as men do, and a women's role is to teach them manners if they are to come into the house. Dorothy is negotiating her reality, as she must.

Dorothy separates from her family, with a bump on the head, as if she is knocked unconscious. Yet, instead they show her go into higher consciousness to explore her psyche, and the dreams of her activity in it. She goes through all this to negotiate her current circumstance. The three men in her environment can also represent the three wise men, with the gifts being attributed to the servant in the castle instead of to them. They are the workers, and Dorothy, trying to establish a sense of how things should be, decides these gifts are needed to adjust their shortcomings. So, in her unconscious, she travels with them and see that they get the gifts they are lacking. Also, she falls and gains attention to show she is of age for puberty and childbearing. The symbols are shown with the crystal ball as Dorothy is learning the facts of life in an illusionary sort of way.

Much of our communication is indirect, and responsibility is gained as we become more conscious of our underlying motives and reasons for our behaviors. The garden may be elsewhere to show the tie to Christianity and the divinity of the manger where baby Jesus is symbolized, representing the humble nature of the environment. This is especially what Aunt Emma brings to it; she depicts the image of a person with a good Christian upbringing.

I believe these values are shown to illustrate that all Dorothy encounters is normal and healthy and to say that a contrary environment is not the cause of what she ultimately deals with. This depiction of the Christian upbringing lends credibility to the average person's search for a better horizon, and takes into account the emotionality and personality of our adolescents once they reach puberty. Dorothy is shown complete with assistance from friends and camaraderie and learning, with the full circle returning to the farm, to show her preparedness, as well as loyalty. She works it out in her unconscious psyche first, and maintains a sense of humility and devotion to her friends and they to her. These are strong messages of the ethics of the middle class culture in America, and we all love Dorothy for it.

CHAPTER FOUR

Spiritual Insights

Who We Are

Who we are is male and female human beings, and as such our motives on a pure level are biological, and that finds its way in expression primarily through emotional outlet. Our physiology can't hide. We have basic shame due to being close to others, due to our human nature. We want to be appropriate, and this is so we can communicate and negotiate our realities without the sexual overtones in the relatedness. Society is set up in a system of roles with the purpose of helping us present ourselves in an acceptable way so as to reduce shame. This is so we can help each other in spite of ourselves, and meet our needs as well. The design is beautiful, and it works, although we are mediating it all the time.

We can best help each other by staying within this system of roles and cues. With the roles, comes a system of cues to assist, and other persons to advise. Our reality is acknowledged outside of us by others, and we do well to listen and negotiate properly since more than ourselves are involved in this process. We can then move into comfortable scenarios of interrelatedness which are designed to not only meet our needs, but to meet the needs society has of us. It is reciprocal in nature. Self-mastery and self-responsibility are eventually learned so that adherence to this system becomes second nature to us. We can then assist others more readily with successful results and desirable outcomes.

The design is beautiful. The fact that it is based on our humanness should not diminish it. We should replace shame with acceptance, and move forward to achieve an understanding of our communications, without the harm of judgment. Then, you will truly love the reality that we have.

Open your eyes and see. It is all in front of you everyday. Just refocus for that perspective. It will amaze you! Life is truly worth living!

I spent years wondering what people were talking about. Then, when I thought I knew, even then there was something more beneath the surface that was going on as well. I observed and listened, but did not hear. I did not know. Not until recently did things finally start making sense. I've had a spiritual awakening that is quiet and calm, yet exciting given the new outlook and understanding of how to interrelate with others. I feel my life makes sense, and I am now wishing I were a younger person so that I could have many more years to enjoy it.

SELF-ACTUALIZATION

I find sometimes that talking and then listening to what I say is helpful in the process of understanding what to do next. When I speak with fortitude and strength, I usually get a response from the environment. For instance, a new person will join the conversation to reflect the feelings I just conveyed. Sometimes I will say things and then someone comes forth and I realize that they were sending communication prior to their appearance. My speaking their words to bring them in is sometimes referred to as channeling. I believe it is frowned upon, or at least the word channeling is, although these dynamics happen all the time. I much prefer their words reflected out. I think perhaps our hierarchy is affected by these phenomenon, with the ensuing power struggle to have this power. Our parents play a role in maintaining some of the dynamics involved in keeping us obedient and quiet, so that our communications are appropriately channeled into productive endeavors such as the workplace, and home environment.

Today I talked to neighbor about going to church. I reviewed my whole situation and ended up explaining my interest in self-actualization. It makes sense that given my interest I would eventually end up interested in Christianity and the church. Christian leaders exemplify the self-actualization principle by virtue of their presence. Society responds with respect and admiration, as well as with money and other adornments. I am wanting friendships and interactions with others so as to maintain my emotional health and well-being, and the Christian church environment appeals to me as safe ground for that. These are my thought processes, yet not necessarily what I end up doing.

Again, I realize that speaking from my real self and saying what I am about is helpful in the process of defining my reality as it appears now. I can redirect in accordance with the person that I am, who is in need of a reflection of my goals and best good. Given that context, speaking my words to say my interests is the most responsible way to proceed. Those are my thoughts for today, as I am in the midst of a struggle of what to do next, or where to go on a daily basis. At my age of 61, busy work to pass the time is contrary to my goals and expectations of myself. I require some sense of commitment so as to feel solid in my goals and endeavors. It is that I seek.

As I write this I see where I am going wrong. For one thing, if I am wanting then I am in need. Starting there, I am off center, out of my real self into my thinking mind. I am thinking all this, not knowing or feeling it. I am feeling scared, perhaps, and I am less than, thinking there is something I must have, and that the church is where it is. I am convincing myself by saying my words, and justifying and defending by including my age and mentioning struggle. I am not aligned with my true self, so my thinking mind has to go through all this until I wake up. And, that is why I do not act on my thoughts, because, on some level, I know all this to be true. My true self is deceptive in that if I am out of alignment with my true self, my thinking self does the work and is who I am as well. Although, I know my thoughts to be thinking about my self, rather than my true self speaking. This helps.

I believe in the adage, close one door and another will open. I am learning to let go of things that do not work, making note of what brought them into my life, and the value at the time. I am then learning to accept the next step, with an awareness of underlying subtle fears and insecurities due to not knowing what that is or where that is. I am happy with myself and ready to move forward, yet hesitant at the same time. So, I define where I am and what the next step is until I am sure of what I am creating. This alleviates some of the anxiety of not knowing. Sometimes the anxiety is heightened as I get in touch with my deeper needs and expectations. There is a complexity about all this that adds to the challenge.

I think the most important learning that I can know is that when I am not aligned with my true self, then I tend to have more insecurities and I act out more. Acting out is when I start just doing things without being sure what the outcome or purpose is. I am vulnerable to acting out because I am not purely following my thinking mind, and I am upset with myself for not being aligned with my true self that knows. I am tired of being a child, as an adult, who doesn't know how to get things done that she wants to get done. I am tired of all the endless steps that are named as ways of attaining a goal. I am tired of thinking I have to go through more just to be and express who I am now. I want to be present, and capable and fully empowered by myself, and yet I also want the acceptance and appreciation of others. I have opened a vortex, so to speak, of desire for attention and I am mediating it with the understanding of the responsibility of maturity. I am ready to act from my true self, and wish to be aligned all the time which is impractical. That thought tempers my anger at myself, so that I am more compliant.

Bucket List

My understanding is that a bucket list is everything that you want to do before you pass on. Since I am now 61 and feeling fatigued and sleepy daily, I am considering my mortality. I have a few things I want to do, and I feel motivated to do them given the situation. My father is 82 years of age, and is writing his book. I am 61 years of age and writing mine. He is a Bible scholar and I am not. I am quite content with my concepts and life experience for my writing. I feel I share on a less-academic level, but with value and worth, just the same.

I feel that I have connected with him on some level in the experience of who I am. I can rationalize and say all the similarities, however, I know the differences too. Should I give up smoking perhaps my health at age 61 wouldn't be on par with his at age 82. He seems energetic and happy and I have been fatigued and depressed. I have started taking medications lately to counteract the depression. They've made me somewhat manic, so I've cut back on that and I am taking adrenal pills at this time to combat stress. My energy seems to be improving already and I am taking walks again.

Another task on the bucket list is the inclusion factor, and seeing that it is included in my life. I was missing my father in my childhood, so I found him and included him in my life. I am still doing that. I intend to bring my relatives together, at least so my son can meet his cousins. I invited my son to meet his grandfather, and that was a successful event. I am continuing to think in terms of including others so no one feels left out like I did when I was young. I may be projecting some of my feelings so I am cognizant of maintaining an awareness of what the rest of the family is doing so as not to project unnecessarily. I am doing this for me, but also for them, so I am remembering to include them in the thought process as well. I want the family to have a sense of camaraderie together at least given our common DNA, if not for other shared interests. This inclusion leads to strength for the individual, and I am personally strengthened by the resolve to make it happen. Including others and sharing our thoughts and feelings about it additionally reinforces the dynamic. Since I felt left out in my younger years, I am repairing my thoughts and feelings so that I feel comfortable wherever I go and with whomever I am with. I feel that the dynamic of inclusion with the family will help increase that probability. I consider it a worthwhile effort and I intend to pursue and treat it as such.

My relations with my family has already improved. My sister and I are talking as if we were old friends, about our childhood and parenting and our failings, and successes. I am amazed, for I was stuck for many years thinking she didn't like or approve of me, and I felt too much judgment about it. I now am finding that I was putting up blocks or obstacles to liking and listening to her, for whatever reasons. I am now able to enjoy a friendship with her that allows us to converse and say what our concerns and parameters are. I am happy about that, and I feel that writing all this has been instrumental in helping me through the process of accepting and liking her, as well as accepting and liking myself. Writing can be therapeutic, especially journal writing but I find that integrating that writing into my relatedness with others is especially helpful. I am growing up.

I am also learning to lift out of the small picture for the bigger picture. I note things said that before may have angered me or caused me to address an issue, but I now go on. I look at the goal that I am trying to accomplish, and I don't let the smaller, insignificant things stop me from pursuing the greater goal. This approach gives me a stronger sense of self, and I feel I am forgiving others for being who they are, just as I would want them to forgive me. Bringing this kind of vitality into my life, allows me to have greater flexibility and fun. I am happier and more well-adjusted as a result.

Pragmatically, however, I do have to address my bucket list so that I am not just in la-la land. I felt that I had to account for some of my life to from my early twenties. I left friends and never actually returned to establish a friendship reconciliation. I located some of my old friends and wrote a letter explaining my life, why I left, and that I have blank spots in my memory. Otherwise, I think I may have checked back with them earlier in life, rather than being prompted to do so by my bucket list. Relationships are important. I know that now, and I understand that NOW is the time to do something about unresolved feelings and endeavors. Otherwise, we end up repeating the dynamics of relatedness with new persons, projecting our unfinished business on them in an effort to resolve the tension. Returning back to the earlier relationships to at least speak to them so that good feelings emerge and people feel worthy is important. We have a need to understand what motivates others, and what we did wrong or right in our relationships. I have sent correspondence and have talked over the phone with my friends about visiting in the next few years. They are interested and responded favorably to the connection and agree philosophically about the conclusions I drew with respect to the relatedness. I feel resolved and happy and peaceful about it.

Now if my boundary issues with my father are responsible for the bucket list, I have to say it is all for the best good. I am happy to have a sense of preparedness for my older age when I am no longer able to agree to travel and meet with others. I see elders and realize how important it is to prepare for old age, especially for those of us who are single. I will stay in the area of my father's environment until he passes, which could be another ten years or so. I will stay so that I feel complete in my sense of duty and responsibility to him, as a daughter, regardless of what his words say. I love him, and I am happy and thankful for the privilege of being his child. That is how I feel.

CHAPTER FIVE

Personality Insights

Not Being Good Enough

Words were said and a dynamic came in today that I must address: the not-being-good-enough dynamic. I talked about my father reflecting on my childhood, and I realized finally that he raised an adopted daughter instead of me. My feelings must have been hurt by this, but I have no recollection of feelings about it. Instead, I think I must have just accepted the message that someone else is more privileged and happy all the time, as she appeared, while I was in sadness and melancholy with my seriousness toward it all. Not saying the things we need to hear, and not working through some of the feelings, or owning the setup and how it appears to others is almost hurtful in itself. That is the lack in my childhood, and the frustration that I internalize so as not to dwell on it.

I feel frustrated that my father and my mother divorced, and that words were not said to explain and help us understand. I am now having to explain and apologize to my ex-husband, and eventually perhaps to my son for similar dynamics that I brought into play as a result. Things were not worked through in my childhood, nor was the family happy with the idea of the divorce. There were lingering animosities that trickled down to the children, and other concerns that were never addressed or met. Shame developed, and needs were not talked about. Lack of ability to talk and communicate with each other and others outside the family was the norm of experience. All this was disheartening. I don't think I came out of it until years later when I started making my own mistakes in marriages. I recognized the similarities to my earlier, divorced family. I guess we don't lose dynamics that easily. Instead, we have to confront the dynamics, at least in ourselves, in order to change them. This level of work takes maturity, effort, and dedication, since our very communications makes these dynamics persevere in our personal and professional lives. What exists, exists, though, and we have a responsibility to understand what that is, should we wish a better reality.

I am analyzing my father's communication to make better sense of him. I recognize that I am a child from a divorced family and that I had an absent father. I guess I am now trying to build him back in so that I feel more balanced with my needs and interests. This is quite a task. I have been a loyal and faithful daughter to the point where now I seem to be acting out just in the expression of my adulthood. I am an adult and wish to be treated as such, and not dismissed. I want my conversations with my father to include me fully as an adult. I don't like that I was falling back into my smaller, personality self where I act as if I don't know what to do. I do know what to do. I am an adult and I am resistant to defaulting to that persona again. It does not serve me, and it certainly does not attract friends, or help. By stating this I am affirming my resolve and thereby making a commitment to myself to stay on task with my adulthood.

Many times I have to go to higher conceptual levels to even interpret my relationship with my parents. This is what I do when things don't make sense on the normal linear levels. My parents don't speak from the conceptual levels I speak of, thereby making things more difficult to discuss if that is not comfortable ground for them. What I mean is that they talk with me with all the dysfunctions that they think I am, and expect that I will respond to that. Communication can be a precarious thing, in that what others expect and want from us is more easily and readily accessed than what we like to believe. Especially from those who control us. Therefore, just talking can be talking to the words that we speak, with all the defenses and pretenses, rather than from the heart saying what is really happening. My frustrations with my parents are what clue me in to the need to analyze further. Once clarified, I then redirect my attentions and say words to reflect the change in my approach so that cognitively it is said and heard. I am growing up and I know that I am responsible for myself and my choices of words and feelings conveyed. This is a helpful reminder of my commitment to myself, and keeps me from giving up. The work is worth the effort.

I guess I kept thinking my parents would speak to me in ways that encompassed my personality, as a grown person. Instead they interact with me in dialogue with the words and never seem to come out of the linear thinking that is said. They seem uncomfortable talking about the talking that we do, and so reframing the conversation so that it is more desirable and satisfying comes from me. I learned from others that two people are present, and I found that transferring that to parent conversations, even at my age, is not an easy task. Parents like to dominate, and when they dominate, I lose my big self. I become smaller somehow. Being the second child, I feel invisible most of the time anyway. I used to be quiet all the time with nothing to say. In college I learned that it was a response to having my words and feelings shut down by another, and I realized how sensitive I was. Now I am fighting back, in a good way, by standing my ground and saying my words and making sure that I know and they know that I exist.

All this is new to me. I notice now so many subtle cues to stop me. I almost didn't believe it. When we talk to others, they usually remark on how we should listen to our parents, and things like that. I have to have a venue for discussing my conversations regardless of what the standard expectation is. This feedback substantiates my vague feelings on the matter. Before asserting myself as a newfound adult personality, I knew I was supposed to act as if I were insecure or inept and needing of attention, as if that is a bad thing. Now where do you think I get those feelings from? Do you think my life shaped me that way and I am just acting out my script? That is the rationale for that behavior. No, I think I am receiving signals and information intuitively about what people need from me in order to appease how they have approached the situation. That is plausible as well, if you think about it. In fact, there could be an entire communication network that is designed and intended to hold us in the pigeon-holed idea of what another thinks and hopes we are. And, it is not said. People do not go around verbalizing that this is what they do. So, therefore, if they don't own their control efforts and the corresponding dysfunctions that it creates in their lives, we would not know necessarily. Then, they would not have to own any responsibility either. That is the amazing part. People like me walk around and we can hardly do anything about it without tremendous ongoing effort toward that end.

I move through all this by restating my intentions and asserting from my big self, I call it, and say what I want to say. I was discussing the issue of inclusion and I guess that wasn't the conversation that my father wanted to have. That might somehow address some of his irresponsibleness from earlier years, and he would rather detour that if he could. Well, with my son, I proactively addressed those issues before he had to opportunity to approach me with it. I wanted to be in touch with him and feel that an understanding was developed about my being absent from his life. I took the time to create space for conversations that would help accomplish that. I still have feelings to mend with him, and he avoids me when he can by not initiating contact. That is how I know our relationship is not fully mended yet. However, with my father, time is shorter. He is 82 years old, and I do not want to take him for granted at this point. I want to be included in his life, and I want him to make space for me as my real self, my big self, if you will, in the relatedness, rather than giving up or giving in to the lesser possibilities. I feel he is not proud of me, and I wish to gain that perhaps. These are important moments in life.

Where to go from here, I am not sure. Venting can be good, but holding the thoughts and feelings to express to another person seems more productive. I find that I am challenging the not-good-enough dynamic and ultimately, it is leading me to my father, and siblings, as society seems to reflect the beliefs that they hold. I might be imagining it, by being focused on their approval, but it sure seems that way. Does life mirror us as we are, or does it show us that which we are not? We selectively see, I am sure, so that what interests us is what we then focus on. So, anything can be true, or not true. So, basically, I state and restate who I am and the nature of my thoughts and feelings until somebody hears me, and realizes that, hey, that is who she is. She is this person that thinks this way and converses about these things. It is lonely if we are not known. We have a responsibility to say who we are, and let others know we know them and who they are. That is the very fabric of society. That is what I endeavor to accomplish.

I am learning to continue to define myself and pay attention to other's definitions of me so that my self- definition doesn't default to just whatever someone thinks. I am learning to assert my person and know that I can hear and understand others, but that I also can be heard and understood. I can display my emotional self as well, and others will come to know and accept that dimension as well. I am learning to define and address every nuance of my personality in order to understand its influence on my psyche, and the overall life that I live. I have learned how to express anger so as to overcome the numbness of not feeling. I no longer wish to shut down when another speaks to me in a way that disables me. Neither do I wish to lash out in protection of myself. I am trying to mediate my responses so that I am more well-balanced. I am better able at determining other people's defenses and denials as well as my own. I focus more on my own behavior now rather than looking outward at others. I notice others, but then I bring the focus back to me to see where my life contains those factors that they bring forth. This is helpful, along with introspection and contemplation, on a daily basis. I feel I am healing, and becoming a stronger person.

SOCIALIZING-IS THERE A HIGHER LEVEL?

Again, I talked about going to church. I reviewed the whole situation, and ended up explaining my interest in self-actualization. Self-actualization is just what it sounds like. It is the fulfillment of one's potentialities, the expression and development of one's talents. I feel that expression of one's self is a way toward this goal. I believe we have the responsibility to express and develop ourselves fully given our understanding of ourselves and society. This is so that we can contribute to society and others in a meaningful way. I say this in conversation so that the idea of full expression of self is said. I do not like to see and know that others are suffering or isolated in their tasks. We all require help and understanding and acknowledgement on our path. We are all human, and as such, require and deserve attention on the level that we need it. Attention is a good thing; it makes flower grow. People are worthy of attention, and our lives are more meaningful when others pay attention to us.

Back to my socializing, though. Why a higher level? Am I trying to escape from my self, my humanness? Or, am I leaving myself out to feel left out? I am doing something that keeps me in a perpetual state of well, maybe I should do this, or maybe I should do that. What is my frustration? I am not working, and due to the audio effects in my thinking brain, I am unable to work. I am on social security disability and I have nothing to do. There is little that I can do about my situation in that regard, except to fill my time with busyness or relaxation. I can clean the apartment only so many times before I find that I am not acclamated to that task. I am bored, and I am wishing to be other than I am, in my plight which sounds pitiful compared to many others. So, I find interesting things to think about that are in the category of fulfilling my potential within the limits and guidelines that I have available to me, and given my resources. I am like many others, in that I can be lazy and yet, I have an internal struggle to deny my situation and attain some great thing to get everyone's attention. Basically, I just want to be known for who I am, and I am not ready to die and give up yet. I want to show myself and prove myself to myself before I go. I want to do and be worthy of the person that I feel I am, and it is this that drives me.

Finding friends on Facebook didn't necessarily prove to be productive. I must mend my relationships and then friendships grow from there. The social networks are more like dating sites anyway, and I am not choosing to present myself to society in that way at this time. Facebook allows me to look at pictures of people with a few descriptive words about them, and then I am supposed to, I guess, decide whether to invite them to be my friend. I cannot do this. What basis can I use? Their appearance, their friends, their family? Am I to start a dialogue until someone responds back, and then find that they are not interested in my in-depth analysis of society and of my parents and siblings? My additional page on Facebook was interesting for a while because I was writing and the public could view my writings and choose to be my friend. This was a nice experience, although it went nowhere in terms of development of friendship.

Then, as it turns out, I had set up what is considered a promotional site that required me to spend money to gain my friends and viewers. That lasted one week. It was a nice euphoria, though, and with Facebook's tally of 4391 views all in a week's time for my $53.85. Friends signed in all over the place, from foreign countries and from the local area. I did, however, shut the site down to keep from continuing to spend more money. That experience inspired me to write this book as a way to speak to the public. So, good came from it. My sister thinks I operate from beginner's brain, which is a way of saying that I jump into the experience without the practical background of information to guide me. I think with that background I might not accomplish the jumping in part!

The friends issue I haven't resolved. How do I find friends at this stage of the game? The either or dichotomy exists as well. I am either seeking out relationship for partnership, or I should put my energy into endeavors at the workplace, or with raising a family. There has to be middle ground in our culture, to make allowances for accomplishing tasks from introspection and contemplation. We must allow time to look at ourselves, not just in the mirror at our physical reflection, and certainly not just to judge ourselves. We must allow time for love of self, to love our neighbors and understand our community. These are necessary tasks that lend toward a meaningful life, and should be cultivated during our younger years so that we can grow old gracefully and happily knowing we have accomplished our task.

I am not looking for a mate, nor am I capable of working in an office at this time, so the middle ground applies to me, now, given my circumstance, and I am taking it seriously. I hope my book will inspire this in others, for it is the only contribution I can think of worthy to make.

THE SHE I AM EMERGES

I am trying to offer more of myself to society to gain back acknowledgment that who I am is known. I may be known as a parent, a wife, and a child, yet the dimensions of my psyche are more expansive and I believe I am trying to convey that message. It is my being outside of the roles and definitions that my family and society have inculcated in me. It is who I know as the person I am that is doing all this, enacting in the roles and appropriate behaviors, then reviewing and deciding on it all, should I be present. I am the person seeing myself do all this. I monitor my self and my behaviors, and direct myself toward the attainment of my goals. I am choosing to be present; in other words, aware of what I call my bigger self. It is more than I am and I know it exists as the potential I can be. This inspires and motivates me to want to grow into my bigger self, just knowing that it exists, and theoretically, I can. My smaller self has outgrown the roles and definitions thus far in my repertoire. My She self desires a greater reality.

So, She is driven to write and explore all possibilities that She does not know until She can find an opening or Segway into a new environment with new possibilities to consider. That is the dilemma I am in, knowing that I aspire to be bigger than the reality that I know how to create that contains me. Now, it is my responsibility to Her to find the next perimeter, if you will, that is representative of what can challenge my new Self. I am to grow into Her, is my understanding of it. I am growing into a new person, and the aspects of who I have been are being reviewed in order to integrate them into the new person that I am allowing myself to become. I am She now, and She is driven to her goal of being included so as to continue her existence. Otherwise, I will have to lay down and die in my old roles and accomplishments, a place where I am just coming out of, a place where my depression held me. That is the place I am leaving, and She is guiding me to new ground. She is my savior, and my guide, and my newfound friend. She is my survival now. This is where I am today. She is me.

I guess I didn't necessarily have to go to church for this spiritual experience. I can rise to new heights right where I am with the thoughts and then the words to create that consciousness. Sometimes this is referred to as creativity. The creative process is where we rework our thoughts, then allow time to reflect and consider, and relax away from our work. Our creative minds solve the problem for us during the relaxation phases. The focused work is tantamount to asking the questions, and the answers come later during rest, with the creative mind processes that we all have access to.

My Self Analyzed

This is a statement from my appropriate, normal self, introducing myself to society given their parameters:

Well, at 61 years of age, basically I come in with concerns of aging and health, women's concerns generally due to my gender, and with psychological interests that cause me to go in-depth to some extent as my expectation for relatedness. Since I've decided Facebook is too impersonal I am meeting neighbors where I live, and considering church as a viable outlet. This will further direct me towards community and perhaps will coincide with my efforts at inclusion. This is my path outlined as I understand at this time.

I am somewhat humble and show that I require direction and advice. I demonstrate an understanding of the lack of interest due to age unless you address a social concern, and attachment issues showing that I use friendships to resolve my parenting and past sibling relationships. I am acting like Facebook isn't good enough, and thereby rejecting a whole sector of people who are on Facebook, and like it. This may be my projecting my not-good-enough personality self since I have been rejected by my family, or at least trivialized by them with that normal approach. Then, I am choosing church as if approval is my aim, due to the values implication with attending church.

I am choosing to be good as if that will get me the acceptance of my family. Then I feel wrong for that or out of place, so I proceed to communicate what my real self is for self-acceptance so that I do not lose my identity in the process of outer acceptance. That is where my spiritual site on Facebook came in. I managed to communicate my inner observations and understandings to the public. This is the part of my personality that seeks expression, and is out of the box my family and others put me in. The Facebook site was my attempt to share who I am to gain true friendships. It includes a higher level need of guiding the public as an outlet of obligation and responsibility that I feel older people have. This increases my value at my age, which is a personal esteem requirement, and fulfills society's obligation of me, given my education and experience. At least that is what I was trying to negotiate by my behavior and choice of words.

I am trying to present myself as I really am, so as not to be misleading. The humble person is who

I am yet I am also the bigger Self that is shifted into when the person that I am construed as is seen as asking for help. I can help myself. I have grown into my adulthood, and so I communicate accordingly to get that message across. I try not to alienate others. My insecurities are sometimes construed as humbleness and not knowing. I am trying to shift out of that more readily so as to have a more accurate presentation that is empowering. This empowerment is vital to my self-esteem, and necessary in order to grow into the person I know I can be. I am, in effect, forcing myself to grow into a larger person, with a greater environment to contain me. I think this is how I move from my humble mother's reality into my empowered father's reality, given my limited perception of the two.

In the past I used to clam up when my feelings were hurt. I was quiet and withdrawn most of the time, and I felt that people were just talking at me. They did not seem to have a sense of what I was experiencing, and I translated that to mean that they did not care. This comes from my early childhood, I am sure. A lot of different behaviors in others triggered this response in me. It wasn't until I was an upperclassman in college that I became aware of the dynamic. I wanted to communicate and not give up and withdraw, and I realized my own responses were the problem. I learned how to be aware when this response would happen, so that I could shift out of it. It was in the way of building healthy friendships and I wanted to change all that. I became aware of some of the source of the hurt feelings and acutely aware of how we unintentionally offend each other daily. My level of sensitivity was working against me, and it would take years before I realized that accepting others and myself as I am was easier if I were to let the hurt go and continue in the conversations. It is the latitude we give others, and that we give ourselves if we are to love and laugh and continue in life.

Now what I am more used to experiencing is the anger reflex. I have only noticed myself once or twice withdrawing from communication due to hurt feelings. I realized it immediately when I did it and I was able to come out of it to communicate. It is a give-up response to another person's inept prodding. Staying inside myself until someone brings me out of it is irrational and never happens. I have to choose some level of courage to address the issues if I think that the other person is inept or inappropriate to me.

The anger reflex kicks in when I address some issues. This is in response to insults that are diminishing to my person. Why would someone want to insult another? I can't know. I only know that we as humans endure many things for the purpose of a relationship, and I am learning to think of the relationship in abstract terms at times. These abstract terms help me decode what the other person is actually doing to me or with me. Thinking in terms of a person only gets me further into the enmeshment of their reality. I am not a doormat, yet if the right person comes along, I could be. That is an indication that I have low esteem issues, and yet that is also the way I am able to work through my personal issues with others, by communicating readily. My anger at myself can only result when things go wrong. Sometimes I find that I am intuiting them and perhaps channeling some of the anger, but that can only be if I am susceptible to that energy organization with anger as a response. So, I cannot blame. That is what I shy away from. We are all instrumental all the time in constructing our realities, and there is no productive use for blame. Remove blame, and denial, and the ability to see and change the hidden behaviors is more likely. Then we can move forward.

So, you see, I diffuse my anger. My own anger is a result of my own inept prodding and my frustration at having an unsuccessful conversation. Anger will only stall the results, and alienate those close to you. It is a signal that there are issues to address, and that can only happen with patience and understanding over time. I understand that now, and regret any and all anger responses, regardless of what I thought I was accomplishing at the time. Other people do not change unless they choose to. I am only responsible for myself and my choices to communicate. I have to remember that since it is so tempting to think if only they would do this or that, but that is unrealistic to think of as an alternative. We have to do our own internal work, and leave others alone. We cannot make them responsible for the responses that we choose. We are responsible for ourselves, and if we are fortunate, others are in our reality.

My Relationships Analyzed

Now, I am left with the emptiness of not having that relatedness in my life, at least not with that particular person. And, all I feel is that I have to spend some time with that person again.

However, he is not interested due to the anger responses I threw at him. His insults angered me. Repeatedly I explained to him the person that I was. I am this person that reads and writes and talks about what I read and write. He wants me to act like a different person to be with him. I enjoy his company, and so since I am a female, I act as such since that is how I experience his interests. I also am an intellectual who wants to work on our relationship. I know he has a resistance to it. We were at an impasse, and anger was what came through me. I think I am angry at falling in love with him. His defense is to act as if we never had the conversation so that he can continue with his own self-serving ideas and approach. I am diminished and have given up the relationship. I cannot continue agreeing to be less than I am.

Yet, a day will pass, and I will be holding myself back from going to see this man again. What is wrong with me? I have thought about extinguishing the behavior that is motivating me to go to him. Now, I am learning to not act on my impulses. We do not have to act out every thought and feeling just because we think and feel it. I am restraining myself. I don't want to get angry again, and I don't want to clam up and just accept it as it is. I want the middle ground, where space is created to talk about these things. I am a person and wanted to be treated accordingly. I am fighting myself.

BACK TO SOCIALIZING ON HIGHER GROUND

What is my goal? What is driving me? What do I want to accomplish? I wish to stay out of the personality level of relatedness in pursuit of true self, and true friendships. I don't need to go to a social environment to start a relationship, and then get enmeshed in their personality manipulations or mine. I am naiive if I think I won't find the same reality again. Replacing someone does not really work. We bring them with us. So, then how do I proceed? I must enter on different ground. The personality self is how I communicate where I am in response to the environment. I am more than what I can express in a social environment. We all are, and that leads me to the next environment, and this book. Perhaps, introducing myself on a professional level will at least show my attempts at disclosing myself on a higher level, on higher ground, for feedback that is more aligned to my true self. This is my task. Others can only respond, or reflect; it is up to us to convey ourselves in accuracy. They cannot do that for us.

The higher ground is social ground as well. I am saying that I want acknowledgement for the entire person that I am. I realize that I desire a bigger environment to encompass my complexities and I understand that I will also have a better choice in the selection process. By changing and improving who I am and how I present myself, I am empowered with the feelings that I may be appreciated for who I really am.

Inevitably, however, life will bring in the mirrors and reflections of what residue is from my past, lingering relatedness, as well as new mirrors to reflect my present thoughts and behaviors. I will have successfully moved out of relationship with one person, yet I am in relationship with life itself. My ego is not in charge. It may be in charge of me, however, outside of me there exists an entire framework of interrelated thoughts and symbols of ideas represented by people daily. This is the abstract approach I mentioned. Organizing your thinking to encompass what reality you perceive as so to perceive a more honest, truthful reality is quite a task. One step at a time, while keeping in mind the overview is helpful. All things work if you work at it.

Given all this perspective, I emerge as more of a spiritual person, yet I believe I am normal like everyone else. I think I merely want to share what I know so that others will have this perspective, with all this information. I have that desire. I know life can be better should we work on it, and I know that I feel all the people I know can be happier, and I want them to be happier. That is some of my motive. To have happy people in my reality.

For most of my life, I was treated as if I had nothing of value to contribute. Others would indicate that they didn't have the time or inclination to hear me out. I am sure this comes from being neglected in my childhood, and it is up to me to change it. So, with sparse feedback, I returned to college, the one place where I received adequate feedback for my efforts. I was an A student, so I developed a stronger sense of self and esteem. I am now trying to transfer that sense of esteem and confidence into a professional ground to get feedback and communications regarding the person that I am. I want to be acknowledged for my insights and understandings, as well as for my spiritual beliefs. I feel these beliefs are true and I have a desire to communicate them for the best good of myself, in saying it, and for others, in hearing it and responding.

This seems simple, yet as I write I go through the frustration of saying what I need to say without talking about anyone. I found that in the act of writing I learned to convert what I thought and felt back to my world so that I gained insight as a result of the process. Now when I talk about them I expect the phone to ring and a whole myriad of dynamics to come in. That keeps me on task to talk about myself and what changes I can do, rather than focusing outward. Once someone else's dynamics come in, then I can challenge myself to interact with their world. It is that simple, yet work is involved.

I am missing a pathway, I think, much as I was missing a father in childhood. I am missing the path to intellectual partners that appreciate my education and my intelligence. The only glimpse I have of that is my father, and he is making himself unavailable to me. I default back to my mother's ground and then communicate with my siblings. When I talk with my sister I understand that I am in my mother's influence, and the intelligent men will not be there. My mother has divorced my father, and she is not willing to consider that option he offers again. Given this, I appeal to the intelligence of my sister and brother to raise the bar to my father's intellectual ground whether he be included or not. I am like my father in DNA as are they, and the dummy-down approach is wearing me out.

I have to proceed with my full self engaged. I do not want my response to hurt feelings to quiet me again. I do not want to be less than I am. I do not want to be dismissed as a child as if I were unimportant, or don't belong. I no longer consider myself a second sibling, wedged in between two other girls. I have attained full authority and autonomy, and my full self wants to be accepted and appreciated as the adult I have grown to be. I want dysfunctional dynamics that others think they need me for, stopped. That is my position at this time.

Due to this, I maintain a sense of hypersensitivity and vigilance in order to proceed in a normal reality. Where are the contrary messages coming from? These are my concerns, and what I know is that every interaction helps to define the next interaction, and the subsequent thoughts and feelings that occur. This keeps me on edge in some ways, yet I have found that I understand reality better as well. In completing what I am missing, I have not. I am still missing the pathway, and I am trying to build the bridge. I have years where I could have visited writer's workshops and networked with intelligent people, but I lacked the skills for pursuing that course of action. My sister has done all that, yet she lacks the desire to write. I found that when I approached my father on my writing task, his response was somewhat with anger and frustration in that he felt I wasn't ready.

He named all the steps in the path that included going to the library and reading everyone else's book. These are the steps I am missing, yet I find they are now obstacles being thrown in my way to say that I am not good enough. Where are the years of cultivating all this in me to prepare me for the ultimate culmination of good writings? They don't exist. So, this is who I am and at 61, with a desire to write, and that advice is no longer applicable.

CHAPTER SIX

Exercising and
Moving Forward

RESIDUE

S o, why am I scared? Why am I hesitant to begin this process? That is what I feel at the moment. Am I sensing resistance and feeling uncomfortable, then not wanting to put myself where my mind wants to go? Am I thinking in a vague, unapproachable way that I won't be accepted for who I am? Or, that the others all know each other, and I am an outsider, so therefore I should go where people I know are? Are these obstacles I am putting in my own way to justify my stay-at-home behavior? Or, are these feelings based on outdated messages I've received my whole life about my unworthiness? Why am I scared? Why am I not willing to move forward? I think it is the uncertainty, the unknown, the newness of an environment that still scares me. I have to move forward; I have to brave it at least to find out. My curiosity and illusion of comfortability have to coddle me forward. This is inevitable.

If my family were there, I would quickly and easily join in. Somehow I developed a dependence on them to be there for me. This I should have outgrown, I think. I have become stagnant somehow. It could be that I've moved too many times to too many locations so that I never was able to go beyond the beginning, superficial aspects of relatedness. This has worked for me in exposing me to differing cultures and developing tolerance toward humanity, in general. However, I am learning commitment now to staying in one place and working through my frustrations there. I am wanting to join in yet I don't really know how. This is an effort for me, and yet I have all the particulars in place, so to speak. I am organized in a mindset for joining in. I have extended this beyond a relationship to meeting my neighbors, offering rides to the store, and being available for conversations.

This sounds good, and is my peaceful place, yet I know all the other battles of my personality. I wish to be more direct, so that I do not have to just be accepting of everyone's way of behaving. I do not wish to take on a male persona, however, I do wish to be more assertive so that I can confront unwanted behaviors that I encounter. I can withdraw yet that pulls me out of the relatedness, and I wish to relate. Perhaps all this communication is interviewing for relatedness. I don't wish to be naive, nor do I wish to trivialize the nature of interviewing, but I do also want to believe that we can talk with others and have it go to a higher ground so it is appropriate.

I am learning to assert myself in conversations so as to update the way to be talked to. This is helpful with family, although others do tend to resist being told how to approach someone. I have to build it into the conversation to maintain tactfulness and sensitivity to the other person present. I am working on my ability to communicate and get along with others. This is my way of not taking others for granted and allowing them to express the specialness that they are, just as I want them to allow me to express the specialness that I am. It is a reciprocal arrangement, and I can't forget that. We all have something to say, and we all have a right to a meaningful life, right now, right here, just as we are. I try to offer that now to others at least by acknowledging same, and by listening. Listening to others is an important part of the task. Role modeling is always a factor, as others do learn from our behaviors. These factors cannot be overlooked. People are more sensitive and fragile that we think. They require care, and care is love and the altruistic love that we can offer to another. My life is enriched by this.

My Family

If I stay to talk with family, I find I am accepted as who they know me to be. Then, I want to be able to bring who I am now to them, and find that they can encompass that. I want to show that I have grown and become better than I was, and I hope that the communication will reflect that. This has to be realistic, for it is accomplished every day by others. I do not always wish to feel that I am replacing them in order to have my needs met. If I join in and yet cannot express what I really truly think then I am quiet, and my psyche is harmed. This transfers to other people and then I am quiet with them as well. I want to learn how to say what there is and I want the others to really hear me. This sounds normal, but it doesn't always happen. I wish my mother were alive so I could talk with her. She never said she loved me until I told her I loved her. At least then she responded. I wish my father were available emotionally to understand and encompass the growing up I am trying to do. He needs to grow up, it seems, and I am then distracted to his purpose. Adult children raising parents is what I end up with.

I have my grievances, but I am tired of them. I wish to move forward and experience things anew. But, I admit it, on some level, I am stuck. I used to easily see that in others, thinking I were forward moving and progressive. Now, I am seeing it in myself, and hoping this tool of writing and thinking aloud with others will help move me out of the mud. I think now that my siblings were intimidated by me when I returned home from college in California. I had a degree in Psychology and I was expounding theories and ideas about how the heavens were as they were, and I was, essentially, full of myself. This makes sense, as I was overwhelmed toward my graduation year with all the possibilities of the next career direction. My family never spoke to that. I was on my own, and now they didn't know what to make of me. I was an alien to them, and they acted accordingly. Upon asking my sister to let me spend the night one night, she remarked that I should call a cab and go to the homeless shelter. So, it is not my imagination.

No, I shouldn't have struck her because of it, but basically I was offended in a way that was outside the norm for me. I rely on family.

My family did not accept nor understand the person that I had become. My idea is that I should be able to join my family as who I am rather than having to revert to earlier personality presentations. I feel that they should be able to help me through the changes I was encountering. Instead they were silent. Perhaps that is where I learned my silent response. They did not take me on, with the challenge I presented. I perceive that as disinterest, and felt neglected as usual. Things did not change because of my college degree; things just looked different for a while. The only interactive approaches were my questions to ask for help to understand the behavior of my siblings toward me. I also counseled my mother and step-father as marriage counseling to help their failing marriage. They needed my strength, not my weaknesses. I began suppressing my own problems and addressing the problems of the environment I was in. I had new skills, and I drew on them to move forward.

We are beyond survival, and we learn every day from the new environments we are in and from the new people we interact with. How can I not show that? And, why can they not accept that, and adapt accordingly? And, if they are unhappy, we can they not express that? My concern is for myself, but ultimately, if I am to be happy and healthy, I have to heal them or deny them. I cannot deny them so I conclude that my family has their own work to do existentially, or the whole thing won't work as well. So, I visit with continual attempts to communicate until I feel something is accomplished along those lines. I want others to heal. I want others to be happy. Can't they see that? I was taught to say all the good things I was experiencing, rather than dwell on the negatives. This kept them from having to take on the responsibility of taking care of some of the negatives in my life. I know that now. They don't have to hide anymore. I don't need their denial. I have grown up. I see the truth.

If I stay and act like I don't know to protect them, I become stagnant and unhappy. I no longer can pacify myself with music and dance, or poolhalls, men and clothing. The material things dazzled in front of me only last for so long before I again begin to delve into my psyche for information to wake me up. I must stay awake, and especially now in my old age, as I jest with puns on the waking up factor. Energetically, I fall asleep due to boredom and poor health, and I must remember to continue exercising as a way of maintaining my youth. All this exists as well. I am this person who is doing all this. I am here trying to create middle ground so that I can negotiate my life. Due to my need to stay within the family's emotional sphere, I am drawn to them for support. Yet then I find I am asking for their approval, when that is not really what I need from them. I need peer relatedness, so that we can experience the joy of sharing who we are with each other. This is important to me. Trying to gain approval is a way of deferring to a lesser personality and hoping they will accept me. I am past that. My communications and emotional self must indicate that by now. I am hopeful and will communicate directly this time. That is my resolve for my mother's ground and with my siblings.

Now on my father's ground I find that normal personality isn't enough so my chances for conversation are limited until I come up with something important enough for him to considering getting involved. It sounds manipulative, but a child has to learn some kind of way to access their parents. I am battling myself on that ground differently since I obviously have to accomplish something more worthy than when I am on my mother's ground. And, my latent anger when thinking about it is that my mother couldn't develop me in accordance with what he might require, but also that he would not spend the time and energy to invest in my development so that I could meet his requirements. And, I am finding out all this at the late date of the age of 61 years old, when it is seemingly almost too late. What career could I possibly develop now, to meet his criteria? And, how many books will he tell me to read so that I can accomplish that? I jest again, but that is the reality of the situation. I was neglected, and I am not allowing it to continue.

Saying the words matters. I don't need the bridge anymore. My sister tried the bridge to learn new activities and develop friendships. I don't want to be her or be my father, and for me, the bridge now represents what others may have. But, I have the desire, and I have the interest in investing in myself in order to develop myself, and I wish to share that with others. I will read everyone else's book later. I will compare myself with others later. I am not necessarily a writer; I am a person who is taking on my life in every aspect so as to have an understanding of its meaning. I want to be prepared to die when it is time, but now I am inspired to share and cultivate and enjoy.

It validates my self-worth to write all this. How I talk about myself and how I allow others to talk to me does affect me. When I listen too much, people get the idea that I am a doormat, even if they don't outright say it. If I talk too much, people get the idea that I am using them. There is a middle ground, a way of balancing conversations so that they are satisfying for all persons involved. It is that that I seek, and I know that others do as well. Staying cognizant of that is helpful. Acknowledging goals and motives is another strategy to moving conversations forward. We do have motives in relatedness and directness sometimes is appreciated. Defining our intent will help us realize how we sound and how others perceive us. There are two people present, and both should be included if relatedness is to occur. If you are clear on your intent and purpose, your communications will reflect that, and results will be forthcoming. Be attentive to what the other is aligned with as well so that there is compatibility in motives. Reflections will guide you if you make yourself aware of that dimension.

Emotional Cleansing

When I jog, even as briefly as I do, I seem to have therapeutic results. I eventually cry but before I do I move significantly through past experiences that I am now letting go of. So, it is always a good cry. Today the topic was the completion of a relationship. After the certainty was over, the significance became clear to me. I wrote a letter to try to illicit a response, and when no response came, my mind was sure the relationship was over. As if the completion had occurred, I left the apartment as if physically I had to leave to symbolize my inner experience. In the car, then, a beautiful song came on and I cried. It was the song from my wedding for my second marriage, and I felt the importance of that event as well while I cried. This represented another leaving and moving forward episode in my life that was significant to me emotionally. I am divorced and somewhat estranged from my child from this marriage. The divorce I accepted, the estrangement I did not. I cried and all the past projected onto my experience in a good way. I was relived of the burden of a relationship that was not the best for me.

I move on.

Now I think of my son and when we separated. I was separated from my father during those same years of age 9 and 10. I have a numbing experience from it and vague feelings of not knowing what the situation was. My cognitions were blank. I now feel responsible for bringing this on to my own child, as I feel I did by leaving him with his dad at age 9. The thoughts in my mind may have been focused on how I should have been raised by my father in order to develop the more important, intellectual person that I aspire to be. This did not help me cope with the separation from my son, except that his dad is a good mom-parent as well. Turning him over to his father, due to my lack of interest in motherhood at the time seemed the thing to do. I did not realize the emotional mistake until later. I cry when I do. He turned out fine, by the way, and is happy and healthy and pleased to be with his father. Boys do need a father, as did I even as a female. My son's dad raised him well in accordance to his culture and with a good environment of inclusion and with a decent work ethic. So, I am pleased. Thank goodness I found a good father who would not abandon his son; he took on the parenting responsibilities and followed through with his obligations of fatherhood in many ways. I am thankful.

I feel better in some ways, yet now I am considering the depression that I was in and what held me there. I am not ready to lay down, so I intend to keep working on this. Paying attention and journaling is giving me insight into the experiences that are necessary to move forward and out of this depression into the empowering person that I can be. How to express that isn't a question, for it is the natural expression of my being should my psychology be in sync with that presentation. My bringing a frame of reference of what I want to focus on helps so that I don't forget when I get caught up in my day to day experiences. Life is less limited than it appears at times. I know that my brain chemicals now suffer as a result of my depression, and I am thankful the medications I take revive me. I have more to offer.

INTERPRETATION OF CAIN AND ABEL

With reference to the Bible, I read the Cain and Abel story and understood the allegorical idea of the representation of the sibling conflict as well as good and evil conflicts. Cain was the good, and

Abel was the wanderer that represented the not-so-good since he left. Cain acted out his childhood projected aggression with Abel. Cain probably was ousted away from his parents to work the fields and resented it. Abel was probably given the attention when Cain was ousted so Cain was able to project his anger at him, knowing instinctively that anger at his parents would threaten his very survival. That is how I perceive the story, although other interpretations exist as well.

I think this because I have an older sister, and I feel she is resentful of me. She is not able to come to terms with her feelings about me, or her father. As a child, I was sent outside to play while she was kept with my mother in the kitchen and with the chores. I had more freedom and independence than she had, although she eventually joined more groups and became more community-oriented than I. I remember through my years of trying to address issues about my mother that I constantly had struggles regarding the thinking of negatives about my mother. It was as if it was taboo. We don't want to lose our mother's love and approval, so how do we grow up? This was a dilemma for a while for me. I didn't want my relationship with her jeopardized, and this is true with many of our relationships. But, we cannot always tiptoe through the mud. I decided that I need the relationship with myself to be strengthened, and I let the other stuff go. I found that the more I loved myself and chose myself over the other, the stronger I did get. This is a powerful incentive to grow into yourself with self-love and responsibility for self being the objective. It may sound selfish but that could easily be a guilt-trip to keep you in someone else's grasp. All this requires contemplation and reflection to stay on task.

THE TENNIS COURT ANALOGY

I remember an encounter with a psychologist while in college. She told me of an analogy using the tennis court as an example to help explain the behavior of my professor. He seemed too aloof to me. Now all I can think of is how aloof I must have seemed being an older student in a class of younger, more personable students. However, at the time I was frustrated with the lack of feedback from the college staff on my progress, and toward plans for my future. The psychologist was giving me perspective on that attitude by use of the tennis court analogy. She said that some people return the ball over the net when you serve it to them. Some do not. Some jump over the net to greet you, and others walk away. I think I have walked away in my life, and I think some of that behavior is learned. I now want someone who is willing to jump over the net to greet me, so I am more forward and direct, and respond to that.

Essentially though, she was a mother-substitute saying your father does not have time for you. Regardless, this higher level way of explaining behavior appealed to me. The physical can be seen, and this way of interpreting applied to human behavioral choices helped me gain clarity. I have to accept the choices of others, whether I like their choices or not. I have to accept that different people respond to different things in different ways. My expectations are only considered, and not the motivating force of their response. The perspective helps me realize that others have their own concerns and parameters and personalities with which to deal. That is what makes the world the complicated network that it is. My psychologist was helping me come to terms with reality. My emotional growth and maturation was being attended to, so as to emerge a healthier, happier and more responsible individual.

Behavioral Dynamics

The communication we encounter growing up pretty much follows us most of our lives. Consider that we internalize our parents and others as we negotiate our childhood. Sigmund Freud said that and more. We learn to mediate the child ego state that desires pleasure called the id, and the internalized parenting so as to retain our adulthood as an individual, named the ego. A healthy ego is important for it demonstrates that we have come into ourselves, fully and completely, as now separate from the parenting and from the needs of the child. Our growth process is complete in some ways, although there is a sense that additional monitoring continues throughout our lives as we negotiate new environments and pathways.

Freud is also known for considering other emotional charges that humans have influencing their behavior, notably sex and aggression. These ideas are fundamental to the beginnings of studying human behavior, as they are an integral part of our humanness. This is primarily a man's perspective, although with today's society, women are included as well. All this is interesting to me, knowing that there is a certain amount of sex and aggression involved in attaining one's best good should internal psychological work be necessary. Others do affect our reality, and it is imperative that we discern what and how that is so that we can have a clear blueprint for the path ahead.

Freud's other important work is reflected in the statement that what is important to us on a fundamental level is our ability to love and work. Love and work are our ways of expressing ourselves so that sex and aggression do not rule us. Our aggressions are channeled into our work at the workplace so that we are productive and know our worth. Our sexual urges are focused on the creation of a family so that we can be proud of our abilities to attract others and take care of them. This enables the possibility of positive feedback from our environment, thereby including us in society. With the inclusion factor, we are satisfied and happy with our reality and the sex and aggression aspects of our nature are transmuted into a happy, prosperous and enjoyable reality. This is the ideal world, and we have the means to create it given the groundwork laid by psychologists like Sigmund Freud.

Conclusion

My father's generation taught us to be quiet unless spoken to or unless you had something important to say. Somehow they manage to never have to talk to us, unless it is a lecture on obeying their rules. And, somehow we never managed to have anything to say. The message was simple: we were not important enough to talk to or spend time with. Expressing yourself was what other people did. For us it was unthinkable to be able to say what we were experiencing without a lot of shame in the way blocking the authentic expression. Since shame is an uncomfortable emotion, and emotions were unpleasant generally, we grew up suppressed and repressed. Since thoughts and feelings were suppressed, observations and emotions were distorted and incomplete due to inadequate thinking faculties, and lack of expression.

My memories of my mother's words were to go outside and play. She never taught me how to help her clean house or how to share in the chores with my sister. I became estranged from my sister later, and now you can see how that could happen. Another memory is of my mother saying to get up in the mornings to get ready for school. She was so cold, as was the floor and the weather during September on the east coast. I think I procrastinate even now when the weather is cold, and I want to lay in bed and think it all a dream I can't interact in. Our experiences affect us. I knew school was there, though, and my grades were good. My mother had to work, and my father was absent. We were latchkey children and on our own most of the day. I have an older sister by one year, and a younger sister by a year and a half. I do not know either one of them very well. We all went our separate ways after our teenage years were over. I feel that my father's influence on our DNA and our childhood helped to cause that to happen. A younger brother was born in later and he seems to visit each one of us in our separate locales. I don't know him very well, either.

I think boundaries are opened to get help from others. Women due to their very nature of dependency open their boundaries to men and others. I am learning how to discern the boundaries of others and myself now. I am finding that I am protecting myself as a result of care I have recently received. I am no longer needing help, having found help, and having learned how to internalize it and help myself, I no longer need to open my boundaries to appeal to others. I have finally found safe ground without and within.

It is because of this, I believe, that I can give to others. Give to others I illustrate by my newfound ability to communicate in a personal way that reaches the other. This is something I could never do before as well. We all know our shortcomings, and can be ruled by them. When changes happen for the better, it is truly a miracle.

I spent most of my life wondering why I wasn't motivated. Why was I so apathetic, listless and uninterested? Sex, music, and clothes interested me as a teenager. Beyond that I had no goals, except to travel back to New Jersey from Texas to visit a past that no longer existed. I eventually figured that out and stopped going there. Since my mother wasn't talking about anything interesting, after my first divorce, I headed to my father's environment in Boston, MA. My father talks a lot is what I found out. That gave me license to speak, or at least the beginnings to get an education to learn what to say so that my words would be important enough to hear. So, that is what I did, although it took the rest of my life to accomplish it. The rewards are there. I am at peace with myself, and others.

Printed in the United States
By Bookmasters